Human Genetics and the Immune System

Human Genetics and the Immune System

Ronnee Yashon and Michael R. Cummings

MP **MOMENTUM** PRESS
HEALTH

MOMENTUM PRESS, LLC, NEW YORK

Human Genetics and the Immune System

First published in 2020 by
Momentum Press, LLC
222 East 46th Street, New York, NY 10017
www.momentumpress.net

ISBN-13: 978-1-94664-656-9 (paperback)
ISBN-13: 978-1-94664-657-6 (e-book)

Momentum Press Human Genetics and Society Collection

Cover and interior design by Exeter Premedia Services Private Ltd., Chennai, India

First edition: 2020

10 9 8 7 6 5 4 3 2 1

Printed in the United States of America.

Abstract

Illness is a part of life. For many years, we have known about diseases. But, we were not always so smart. The Black Plague ravaged Europe between 1347 and 1352 and killed 30–80 *million* people. No one knew how people caught the condition and lots of ideas failed. People just died. But, not everyone died; possibly, their immune systems helped them fight off these *invaders*.

Today, we know about bacteria, viruses, cancers, and other invaders, and we usually let them run their course. That is because our bodies detect and fight them. That is immunity.

Keywords

Immune; bacteria; inflammation; lymphocytes; antibodies; antigens; vaccinations; blood types; AB; BB; AA; AO; BO; OO; rejection; transplantation; cadaver; living donor; HLA; cirrhosis; autoimmune; immunodeficiency; allergies; anaphylaxis; immunogenetics

Contents

CHAPTER 1

General Information

Most of us do not think about the immune system, but it works defending us and keeping viruses, bacteria, and pollution at bay. History shows we have amazingly improved. From the times of the Black Plague (see Figure 1.1) where doctors wore masks to keep from getting sick, today, we have medications that boost and slow down our immune systems.

Figure 1.1 Plague Mask Worn by Doctors During the Black Plague

Active immune cells, B cells and T cells develop as white blood cells in the bone marrow. They both are lymphocytes. While B-cells mature in the bone marrow, T-cells travel through the bloodstream to the thymus gland—a small organ between the lungs and behind the sternum—and mature there.

This could explain where early in diagnosis of leukemia samples of bone marrow was taken from the sternum.

When your doctor takes a blood sample for testing, you may wonder what he or she is looking for (see Table 1.1).

If the numbers are low: serious anemia can cause a lack of oxygen and is treated by iron supplements or transfusions if necessary.

Table 1.1 Components of blood

Test to find	Purpose	Normal	Abnormal
# of red blood cells	Carry oxygen to cells	4.1–5.1 million	High: Low: Anemia
# of white blood cells	Fight invaders (T and B cells)	45–10,000	High: active infection Low: difficulty healing
Amount of hemoglobin	How much oxygen is carried.	14–17 g/dl	Oxyhemoglobin carries the oxygen to the cells. Low: not enough oxygen goes to cell

If the number is high, it signals that there is an inflammation (infection) or if very high it might indicate Leukemia.

If the number is low, might need a study of lung function to see if the problem is there.

CHAPTER 2

How Does the Immune System Work?

The immune system has three levels of protection.

First, the *skin* is a barrier to bacteria and viruses; its cells are called epithelial cells; they are the outside layer of the skin (if a cut occurs, invaders can enter).

Second, an *inflammatory response* to the invader, triggers the killer and helper T-cells, and killer T-cells destroy the infected cells. They recognize the infected ones by the molecules on the cells called antigens. The cells are marked, and the killer T-cells destroy them.

Healthy cells have *self-antigens* on the surface of their membranes. They let the T-cells know that they are not intruders. If a cell is infected with a virus, it has pieces of virus antigens on its surface. This is a signal for the killer T-cell that lets it know this is a cell that must be destroyed. When the killer T-cell fits the antigen receptor, poison is released (cytotoxin).

Third is the *adaptive immune system (specific targeted responses)*. It contains cells specifically made to identify and destroy foreign cells. Antibodies trap the invading viruses or bacteria in large clumps. This makes

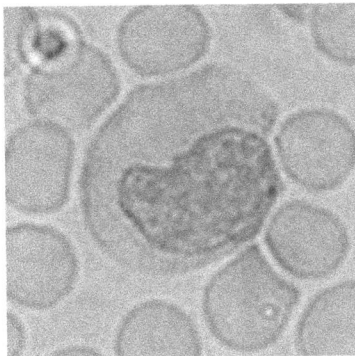

Figure 2.1 This is a microscopic photo of a lymphocyte surrounded by red blood cells

it easy for macrophages to eat them. Antibody-coated viruses are called *neutralized* because they cannot infect your cells.

Even after you have fought off your infection, some antibodies stay in your blood. If that virus tries to infect you again, your immune system has a head start trapping it.

How Does Immunity Work?

Toward the end of each battle to stop an infection, some T-cells and B-cells turn into memory T-cells and memory B-cells. As one would expect from their name, these cells remember the virus or bacteria they just fought. They live in the body for a long time, even after all the viruses from the first infection have been destroyed. They stay in the ready mode to quickly recognize and attack any returning virus or bacteria.

Once an invader enters the body, protein molecules on the invader cell (called antigens) activate the immune system.

First, the detection of an antigen stimulates the T4 helper cell, which then activates the B-cells.

The activated B-cells then divide and produce proteins called antibodies.

Once the B-cells are activated and released, they bind to the antigen wherever it is found in the body. Binding marks the cell for destruction by other cells of the immune system.

Another interesting fact is that some activated B-cells become memory cells and can start a massive response if the antigen enters the body sometime in the future.

Note: Vaccinations are based on this fact. They include inactive (attenuated or weakened) form of antigens and trigger an immune response.

CHAPTER 3

Blood Types

Blood Typing

Before DNA, another form of blood typing was used in transplantation and other immune system problems.

A little review:

The best known blood typing system in humans is called ABO. The alleles (genes) that lead to any blood type come from the mother and the father.

Half of the genes come from the mother and half from the father.

A blood type is determined by these genes and how they combine. To understand this, refer to the following:

Blood type A has the alleles AO or AA.

Blood type B has the alleles BO or BB.

Blood type AB has alleles AA and BB.

Blood type O has the alleles OO.

Blood types do not change after birth and can be identified with a simple blood test.

You may be familiar with these blood tests in paternity testing or in your own medical checkup. When the question of paternity exists, blood tests are taken of the mother and baby and, if needed, matched with any possible father's blood.

Therefore, any of the following combinations, mentioned below in Table 3.1, can occur:

Table 3.1 Possible gene combinations that can occur with blood type genetics

Mother	Father	Genetic combination from two parents can be the following
AA	BB	AB
AO	BB	AB or B

Table 3.1 (Continued)

AB	OO	A or B
BO	BB	B only
BO	OO	B or O
OO	OO	O only

Blood types are used for determining whether samples are match types for blood transfusions and identification. If the wrong blood type is administered, the immune system will attack cells and cause a phenomenon called clumping (see Figure 3.1). If the wrong blood were transfused it would cause a great deal of damage and possibly death.

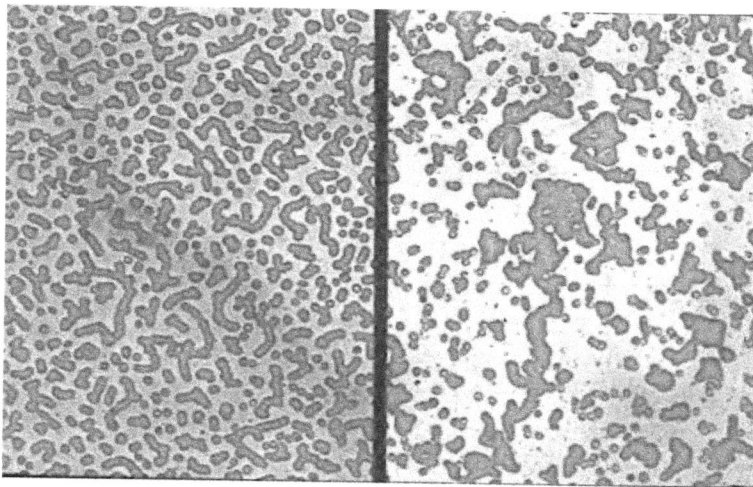

Figure 3.1 Blood Test: (Left) Normal, (Right) Clumping

In this chapter, we are interested in how blood types are used as a preliminary test to begin finding a match for a transplant.

Before DNA, only blood type was used in finding a donor. It was not perfect, but, initially it could separate out the possible donors and non-donors. Family members were the first tested because they had similar genes as their siblings.

The immune system will reach out for any cells with a different antigen, not necessarily a disease. On a large scale, an entire organ (kidney and others) would make a perfect target for rejection. But, many people have had transplantations and live healthy lives (see Chapter 4).

Although significant information is known about the immune system, we have not reached a time where organs are interchangeable.

CHAPTER 4

Transplantation

When an organ fails and is needed for life, it can sometimes be treated by medication (for example, if the thyroid gland is removed, a synthesized thyroid hormone can be taken in a pill form). But as an option, a donor thyroid may be used.

Table 4.1 Organs used for transplantation

Living Donors Can Only Be Used With Certain Organs**

Organ	Obtained from	Condition
Kidney**	Living or cadaver	Severe kidney disease
Pancreas	Living (partial) or cadaver	Cancer or damage
Lung**	Living (lobe) or cadaver	Lung cancer, pollution
Liver**	Living (lobe) or cadaver	A healthy liver can regrow.
Heart or heart and lung	Cadaver	Obviously, no one can live without one.
Bones**	Cadaver	Funeral homes donate, but if donor had cancer, it would begin growing in the recipient
Bone marrow**	Living	The bone marrow will begin making new healthy red cells and lymphocytes after it is transfused into the patient's bone marrow.
Skin**	Living or cadaver Self-donation	Usually, for burn victims, doctors can use skin from the patient. We now can grow tissue in the lab.
Cornea**	Cadaver	

The availability of actual organs for transplant varies all the time due to a lack of available organs (we will look at this later in this chapter). If a match is made, then surgery must be done almost immediately after a donor dies.

Who Might Be an Organ Donor?

The perfect donor is a young, healthy, and dead individual. Sounds strange, but a perfect person who fits this description is a motorcyclist. In a crash, the head hits the pavement, and many riders do not wear helmets. Because brain death is necessary for organs to be removed, these serious motorcycle accidents usually involve the skull and brain. Even in such a situation, the family can refuse.

Let us look at some other problems associated with organ donation. Think about what you might want and who to tell about it.

Table 4.2 Scenarios about transplantation and donating organs

		Decision 1	Decision 2	Another possibility
Scenario A	A child dies and the parents will not allow transplantation of his or her heart. They are told these are the hardest organs to find due to their size.	Parents refuse. The fetal heart is removed and kept in stasis until a recipient becomes available (time is important).	Parents agree after a doctor tells them how many babies are in need of hearts at birth.	Before any decision is made, the story is released to the press. Often, a court might decide if it is right to remove the heart[1] under these circumstances.
Scenario B	A young man dies in a motorcycle accident and his brain is not functioning when he is brought to the emergency room (ER).	After looking for next of kin, the hospital gives up. The organs are never harvested.	In order to avoid a law suit, the hospital takes a new step and asks a judge to decide.	They keep him alive for a while until a recipient is found.

---

[1] A case not long ago involved a patient with a few relatives who did not want to release his organs for transplant. No one could decide. The relatives searched his home and found a note stating what he wanted. The organs were harvested.

What if they did not find the note?

Scenario C	A woman is brought to the ER and cannot breathe on her own; the doctors put her on a respirator and call the family: husband, mother, and father.	Her family rushes over to speak to the doctor. No one can agree. The husband says she told him not to use a respirator, the parents say to keep her on the respirator.	A judge is asked to do the decision making. He or she decides that her husband had her consent (not written, but verbal). The organs are removed.
Scenario D	In the ER, a person dies and no *next of kin* can be reached. But, his organs are healthy.	The hospital has very few patients who could no donate or remove his organs with no one's consent?	The need for organs is dire (see the following statistics)

Legal Rulings: If a person is comatose and connected to a respirator, or dead from an accident, the *next of kin* must decide. Some hospitals want a written form with signatures, while others just need a verbal consent.

Who is the next of kin? Parents, spouse, children (for elderly), and for small children, parents. Most states follow this format. Big problems can arise when relatives do not agree.

Why? Because doctors and hospitals will be sued if this is done without consent. This is a fine line because the organs may work and save the patient.

Why Do People Refuse Organ Donation?

1. They want their relative to be buried intact. Usually, a family or religious tradition causes this.
2. Cost (if not paid for by the donor's family).
3. They think that doctors are not trustworthy.
4. They know about donation and wonder how the organ will be obtained.
5. How could they ever repay the family of the donor.
6. They wonder if their relative might recover.

How Do We Overcome This Gap?

There is a huge gap between donors on the transplant list and people who need organs; something should be done, and here are some suggestions that have been offered:

(a) Give the doctors the right to harvest organs if there is no next of kin.

(b) Allow payment for the organ.

(c) Make it easier to sign up to be on the transplant list (advertisements[2]).

(d) Change the law so that we begin carrying donor cards *only* if we *want* to donate (called presumed consent). More details are covered next.

(e) Presumed consent already in place in BELGIUM, SPAIN, UK (2020), THE NETHERLANDS.

(f) Allow donors to check their own family for matches.

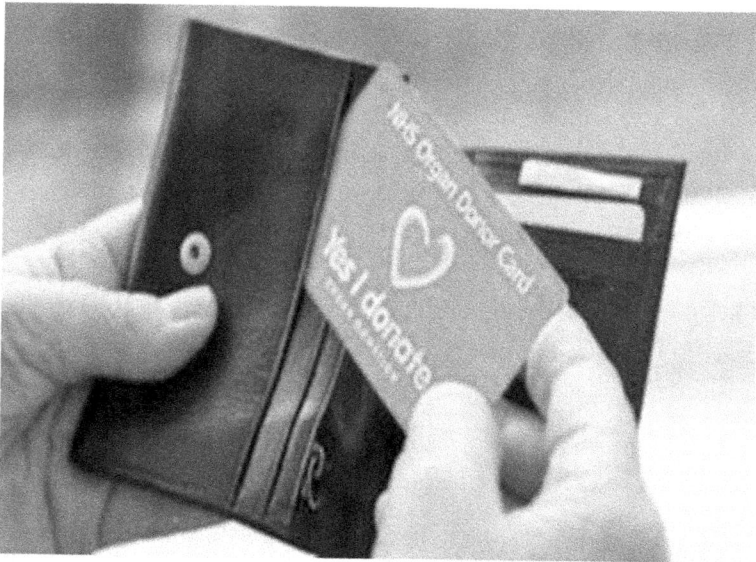

Figure 4.1 This card is issued to those who want their desires made clear to doctors and paramedics

---

[2] In Hawaii, there are ads that run a lot, showing young people during different things (surfing, picnicking, and so on). Each looks up and says "CHECK THE BOX." Next, the video explains the box on your driver's license.

What Can Cause a Patient to Need an Organ?

Table 4.3 What conditions can lead to a transplant?

Needed organ	Condition	Other information
Kidney	Chronic kidney disease, missing kidney, accident	Certain kidney diseases are inherited. Anyone can live with only one working kidney.
Pancreas	Cancer, accident	Often damaged in car accidents
Lung	Lung cancer, chronic obstructive pulmonary disease (COPD)	Of course, smoking is a cause, but pollution and exposure to chemicals at work (asbestos) is serious.
Liver	Cirrhosis, alcoholism, liver cancer	Serious drinking and/or cirrhosis caused by liver cell death*
Heart	Serious heart attack, weak heart	Absolutely no living donor qualifies here, but if the transplant fails, a new heart must be found as soon as possible.
Bones	Amputee, infections in bone	These types of transplants are normally safe, but if the donor died of cancer, it is passed on.
Bone marrow	Leukemia and other blood diseases	Bone marrow with new blood making cells are given to the recipient.
Skin	Burns, accident	Create new tissue in lab or get some from the burn lab.
Cornea	Cornea missing due to accident	Replace
Uterus	If not damaged, it can be used.	Babies have been born from a woman with a transplanted uterus.

How Are the Recipients Chosen?

Tissue match: Human leukocyte antigen (HLA) (see Figure 4.1), blood type, and the health of the recipient are considered. Close relatives are good donors; the best are identical twins.

When transplantation first began, doctors knew that organs were not compatible between people, but the knowledge of genetics was limited. Even before that, pioneers were looking into familial donors and found that transplants between siblings and parents worked better.

But, medical professionals knew that identical twins were exact copies of each other because they came from one fertilized egg. So, it made sense that their organs would be compatible, but it took a doctor with a reputation to try it: Dr. Joseph Murray.

Here is his story:

Richard Herrick received the first successful organ transplant in 1954. He entered Brigham and Women's Hospital in Boston suffering from kidney failure. His brother, Ronald, an identical twin, volunteered to donate a kidney to Richard. Ronald just wanted to help his brother. The night before the surgery, Richard wrote a note to his brother that read: "Get out of here and go home." Ronald wrote a reply: "I am here and I am going to stay." The transplant was successful, and the surgeon, Dr. Joseph Murray, was awarded a Nobel Prize for this medical breakthrough.

Ronald Herrick went on to become a teacher, while Richard married and had two children. Unfortunately, eight years after the transplant, Richard died of an infection in the transplanted kidney. He was 69 in 2010.

Figure 4.2 Herrick Brothers After Surgery

But today, we have much more information about the genetics of a transplant and drugs to calm the immune system after transplant. Drugs that stop rejection, slow down the reaction of the immune system, so it will not attack the organ.

Calming the immune system can be dangerous because we lose some our defenses, and other invaders (colds, pneumonia, and cancer) can enter and not be detected.

Also, scientists have found a group of genes (HLA) also called histocompatibility complex. It is a group of genes found on chromosome 6 (see Figure 4.3).

We discussed blood types in Chapter 3; for many years, blood type was all we had. With the explosion of genetic information, now we can make it possible to actually map chromosome 6.

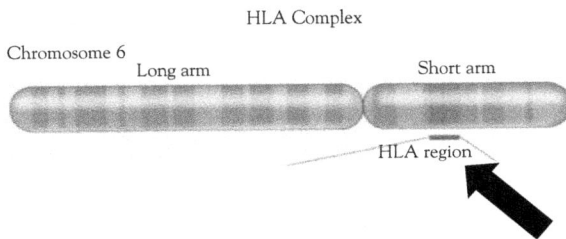

Figure 4.3 HLA Complex on Chromosome 6. At address 6P21 (see arrow) Meaning
Note: If the use (and misuse) of this chromosome interests you.
Read: Chromosome 6 by Robin Cook.

On chromosome 6 on the P arm (short arm) at region 21.
Chromosome 6 showing where the HLA genes are carried.
6P21 Genetic Address

Histocompatibility

The following things are taken into consideration (but not binding) when organs are transplanted. What organ is needed? How ill is the recipient? Is the donor healthy (living donors)? What is their age? What is the medical condition?

And, an HLA match (see Figure 4.3)

Can doctors take your organ if it is needed for a seriously ill patient?

Can you sell your organs? Well, the answer is Yes and No.

In most countries, it is illegal to sell organs or buy them. With the extreme shortage of organs (see the Table 4.4), selling organs seems to be sensible, if it is kept to organs from living donors with their permission.

What are some of the drawbacks of putting organs up for sale?

Note: A number of years ago, a woman put her kidney on Craigslist. She did not know that this was not allowed by Craigslist. So, they removed the ad. In the four days it was up online, she received 15 e-mails.

Poor communities would benefit with funds paid, but might be taken advantage of.

What are some of the advantages? As long as the donor understands everything, this could be done. And, it has.

Does it violate any existing laws? In some countries, this is illegal. But there may be a black market.

Who benefits? (Donor? Recipient?) Everyone.

If the donor is already dead, should the relative get paid?

Which countries still allow payment? Israel and Holland are discussing this;

China, too.

Statistics from: Organ Procurement and Transplant Network website, 2019

Table 4.4 shows some statistics on organ donors and recipients.

Let us analyze these statistics; yes, they are only numbers, but we can examine them closely and answer a few questions.

As we look down columns 1 and 2, what do we see? As years changed, so did organ donations. Why? Education of consumers? Advertising?

The number of transplants slowly increase, the number of patients on the waitlist shoot up. Why?

The numbers of donors seem to stay the same. Better informed doctors and patients?

If only 13,821 people donate, why are there twice the number of transplants? Can more organs be transplanted? Do recipients need more than one?

Table 4.4 Transplantation over the years

Year	Number of donors	Number of transplants	Number on waiting list
2001	12,702	20,314	79,524
2002	12,821	21,523	80,790
2003	13,285	22,026	83,731

2004	14,154	23,266	87,146
2005	14,497	24,239	83,731
2006	14,750	24,910	87,146
2007	14,400	25,473	90,526
2008	14,631	27,040	94,441
2009	14,149	28,118	97,670
2010	14,011	28,940	100,775
2011	14,257	28,366	105,567
2012	14,412	28,964	110,375
2013	15,062	28,458	112,816
2014	15,947	28,662	117,040
2015	16,473	28,539	121,272
2016	17,554	29,534	119,364
2017	16,473	30,973	115,759
2018	17,554	36,529	113,759

What about animal donors? (No written consent needed.)
Not all animals can be donors for humans, the closest are the great apes. But, as you might expect, the United States does not allow such transplants, except in clinical trials, and Food and Drug Administration (FDA) approval is needed.

We already have made some big forward steps:

(a) Animal parts are used to substitute for heart valve (porcine/pig).
(b) Animal tissue (porcine) is injected into the brains of Parkinson's patients these cells can produce dopamine.
(c) The doctor will need permission to remove the human organ and inform the recipient, if it fails, with an explanation about animal's tissue compatibility.

Pig organs have other problems; porcine viruses may enter with the transplanted animal organ, and because the patient already has a compromised immune system, these viruses might activate.

In some heart transplants, tests have been done with a new idea: chimeric immune transplant. In this method, pig bone marrow is injected into the human bone marrow. When this happens, the recipient would not reject because the pig immunity would not trigger the rejection. However, this is still being studied.

A story about xenotransplantation: an interesting story occurred on October 14, 1984, when a baby (baby Faye) was born with a hypoplastic left heart syndrome and needed a transplant to live. The problem was the shortage of tiny hearts, and Dr. Leonard Bailey had been working for years with apes. He spoke at length to Baby Faye's parents about using a baboon heart, which was the closest in size. When they gave permission, there was an uproar, but they stood their ground.

Years later, when asked for a copy of medical records, the hospital did not release them.

Results: Baby Faye died after successfully using the baboon's heart for 20 days. For some (Dr. Murray), this was very successful. But, to others, it was unthinkable to put your newborn (or a baboon in such a situation).

Were these parents wrong?

Other examples of animal donors in use: pig heart valves have been successful.

After a transplant, drugs will be administered in a difficult schedule for the rest of the recipient's life.

What if Rejection Occurs?

Because organs from one person might be attacked by the recipient's immune system, two things could be done to counteract the rejection:

1. One, remove organ and replace with another on the donor list.
2. Two, immediately begin anti-rejection drugs and keep changing the dose.

In retrospect, this might mean, the organ originally transplanted was not a good match.

The side effects of the anti-viral drugs might be too much for the patient to use.

Table 4.5 Anti-rejection drugs

Drug name	Side effects
Prednisone: steroid	Fluid retention, weight gain, fatigue, increased blood sugar, stomach irritation, irritability and increased alertness, and hunger
Tacrolimus (used in liver and heart transplants)	Abnormal dreams, agitation, frequent urination, general feeling of discomfort or illness, itching, skin rash, joint pain, loss of energy or weakness, and mental depression
Cyclosporine antibiotic	Shaking, high blood pressure, infection, headache, nausea, and excessive hair growth
Mycophenolate Mofetil (CellCept) antifungal	Nausea, swelling, rash, headache, and increased heart rate
Imuran (Azathioprine) can increase chances of cancer, used with auto-immune	Nausea, vomiting, diarrhea, and hair loss
Rapamune (Rapamycin, Sirolimus) used after a kidney transplant	Tiredness, vision and hearing problems, weakness, and bone pain

CHAPTER 5

Autoimmune Diseases

In previous chapters, we have looked at how the immune system protects us by identifying foreign substances, viruses, and bacteria, targeting them for destruction. But, what if a donor organ is inserted in the body with foreign cells?

The same exact thing! You are probably thinking this can be tackled (see Chapter 4).

But, why does the immune system begin to attack our own cells?

The immune system is controlled by several groups of genes. The study of these genes and how they function is called immunogenetics. They encode for proteins on the cell surface as well as the antibodies that directly attack foreign antigens. The receptors on the surface of our T- and B-cells are also encoded in our DNA. Understanding how these genes and their respective proteins work has helped us cure infectious diseases, prevent infection, and make organ transplants possible.

Because these genes control the immune response, mutations in these genes can also cause diseases of the immune system, including autoimmune disorders, and allergies.

Diagnosis of autoimmune conditions has been difficult in the past; there was often no way to diagnose. But now, there are treatments, along with knowledge about the DNA of viruses and bacteria; in addition, they can be overcome with steroids. This treatment works temporarily because of the toxic side effects of the long-term use of steroids.

Treatment here is similar to other conditions such as human immunodeficiency virus (HIV) (see Chapter 6) and acquired immune deficiency syndrome (AIDS).

In autoimmune disorders, listed next, the body fails to recognize its own cells and attacks and destroys them (this includes juvenile diabetes, arthritis, multiple sclerosis (MS), and inflammatory bowel disease). See Table 5.1.

When you look at this list, you are probably familiar with some of the listed disorders. Conditions marked with a * had a questionable diagnosis, but as we learned more about autoimmune condition, more scientists are working on it. In autoimmune disorders, listed next, the body fails to recognize its own cells and attacks and destroys them (this includes juvenile diabetes, arthritis, multiple sclerosis (MS), and inflammatory bowel disease) (see Table 5.1).

Do you know anyone who has one of these conditions?

Table 5.1 List of autoimmune diseases

	Area affected	Symptoms	Treatment
Allergies	Skin, other organs	Cough, breathing problems, asthma	Antihistamine Decongestant Leave allergen
Rheumatoid arthritis	Central nervous system Joints	Pain Additional symptoms from other inflammational areas	Steroids, pain killers
Psoriasis*	Skin	Red and scaly patches	Steroids, creams. Immunosuppressants
Narcolepsy*	Sleep center of the brain	Falling asleep many times a day	Drugs to stay awake, caffeine, psychological
Diabetes (Type 1)	Pancreas	Very high and low blood sugars	Insulin, diet, regimented schedule
MS	Central nervous system	Begins in your 20s	Steroids, specific immunosupression drugs
Graves' disease	Thyroid gland	Increase in thyroid hormones	Removal of the thyroid
Celiac disease*	Digestive system	Diarrhea, cramps, bloating, Mouth sores	Gluten-free diet. Mitigate symptoms, check drugs to control symptoms*
Crohn's disease	Digestive system	Same	Same
Lupus* erythematosus	Joint pain, weakness, hypersensitivity to light	Systemic: bones, skin, and kidneys	Steroids, treat symptoms

Alopecia*	Hair follicles	Clumps of hair fall out	Hair follicles die and wig is a must. Steroids
Pemphagoid	Skin	Hardening of the skin, liver involvement	Steroids, Anti-immune
Scleroderma	Skin	Same	Same
Fibromyalgia*	Pain in the endings	Pain all over the body	Control pain. Rest, lower stress
Guillain–Barre syndrome	Partial paralysis of face and other parts	Not much treatment, but it clears up by itself.	Muscle relaxants Stress relief
Restless leg syndrome*	Movement of legs while sleeping	Mild sleeping pill	Movement of the legs while sleeping, hard to stop pain when you awake.

The Autoimmune Spectrum

The symptoms of an autoimmunity can continually become worse without treatment of some kind. The progression of the illness can be calculated by using the following illustration:

As time goes on, more symptoms surface and increase in intensity.

No inflammation → 1–2 symptoms → 2–4 symptoms → 3 or more symptoms

Figure 5.1 Diagnosis of Auto-Immune Conditions: The more symptoms, the more serious the diagnosis, and as the frequency (days per week) increases it worsens it

CHAPTER 6

HIV and AIDS

The topic of human immunodeficiency virus (HIV) and acquired immune deficiency syndrome (AIDS) has been in the news for quite a long time. At one time (1980s), it was much more than a medical problem. It pulled in all the parts of our political and personal lives. In some areas of the United States, it also brought out prejudice and anger.

What Is the Difference Between HIV and AIDS?

HIV is a virus, also called human immunodeficiency virus. Specifically, this virus attacks the cells that make up the immune system. If untreated, it will eventually spread, causing AIDS (acquired immunodeficiency syndrome) and death.

In the early years of HIV, doctors noticed rare conditions that they had never seen before: a form of pneumonia (pneumonia carnii) and a form of cancer (Kaposi's sarcoma). These are sometimes called AIDS-defining illnesses because when the virus (HIV) attacks the immune system which, in turn, can *not* kill the HIV viruses already in a cell, and the cell dies. These diseases are extremely rare; if a patient has one, it alerts the physician to look for AIDS.

Human Immunodeficiency Virus or HIV

All viruses work by reproducing themselves inside a healthy cell. Then, the cell breaks open and all these viruses move throughout the body, and HIV is no exception in IV. This also kills the T-cells, and when the number of T-cells are low enough, HIV becomes AIDS (see Figure 6.1).

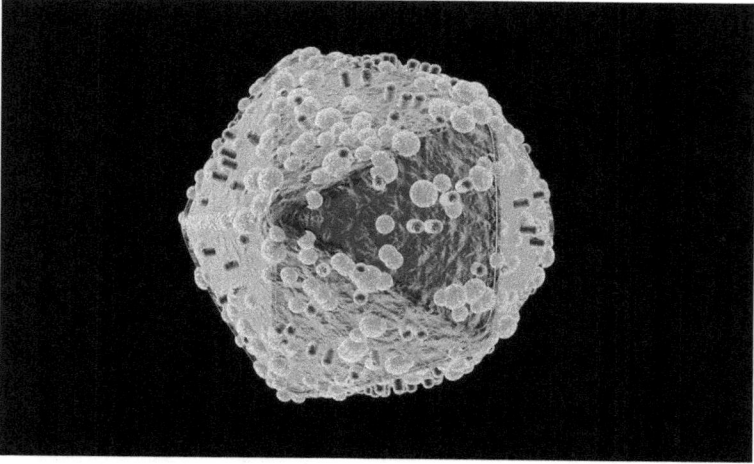

Figure 6.1 This is a photomicrograph of the HIV virus

When the white blood cell (WBC) count drops down, certain diseases (opportunistic diseases[1]) and symptoms show up because the body's immune system is compromised. As the HIV-effected cells increase, even simple diseases become life-threatening (for example, cold).

HIV has a long history before and after the treatment was available. The treatment was sped up because of organizations such as ACTUP (AIDS Coalition to Unleash Power) forcing the Food and Drug Administration (FDA) to speed up the process of releasing the treatments.

It took a while, but after the treatment was released to doctors and then patients, they were *quickly* used and saved lives.

If not treated, over time, the WBC count drops lower and lower and death occurs from other diseases.

How Does One Get HIV?

After much discussions and statistics taken at the time, it seemed there were a number of ways: sexual contact, blood transfusions, organ

---

[1] These are rare because only someone with a compromised immune system can have them. Some examples are pneumocystis pneumonia, thrush, and Kaposi's sarcoma (a form of cancer).

transplants, blood products, and any other contact with blood.[2] But *not* kissing, touching, or sharing food. This turned into a full-blown panic in the United States; people were making illogical choices, with no real knowledge of the condition. For example, many thought *not* using dishes or cups from HIV-positive people, they would stay safe.

Read the case of Ryan White in the next chapter.

Problems with Diagnosis

At first, the United States had a few cases of a rare form of pneumonia (pneumositsis carnii), but it began to show in certain groups. The way it was treated and diagnosed was a surprise because it was so rare, and so doctors began to discuss this and discovered that it had been found in certain groups such as homosexuals, Haitians, children born from infected women, people who have had blood transfusions with HIV-infected blood, and hemophiliacs.

As this sometimes happens (as we all know), the truth has problems being explained, and panic occurs. Some examples were people were fired from jobs or not hired, just because they were part a group that was affected. It also was suggested that, if a patient tests positive for HIV, he/she should be confined to a specific area of the country. Read case of the DEVIL.

---

[2] A dentist who was HIV positive passed the virus to a number of patients, without telling them he was HIV positive. This was not only unethical, but also illegal, and things just escalated from there.

CHAPTER 7

Milestones in HIV

Case I: Saving the Devil

Researchers in Australia came across a seemingly unrelated case.

Not so many years ago, a rare mammal was found on the island of Tasmania (near Australia). This island was small, but had many rare species due to its isolation.

Enter: The Tasmanian Devil (yes, this is also a cartoon character).

Over the years, population of Tasmanian devils dwindled. The cause seemed to be cancerous tumors growing on their snouts.

Australian scientists went to study the disease that was wiping out the Tasmanian devils (see Figure 7.1). Cancer? Really? How did they get this virulent, deadly disease? It was communicated from one another.

If someone with cancer BIT your nose, would you get cancer?

No

Cancer is not communicated in this way with humans.

Figure 7.1 Tasmanian Devil

The study noticed the tumors were always on the side of the snout, and the devils died quickly. During this time, the scientists watched them mating and saw an amazing thing. During sex, the male bit the female on the snout, almost exactly in the place where the tumors would grow.

The keepers wanted to isolate those with the cancer to stop the spread and the ultimate extinction of the devils.

What does this have to with the human immunodeficiency virus (HIV)? On a much larger scale, HIV was killing people, certain groups of people. If those groups were put in an area by themselves, would this isolation possibly work and make others be safe?
Didn't this work with leprosy?

When HIV first became an epidemic, it was found mostly in men. They were of four groups: homosexuals, Haitians, drug addicts, and people with hemophilia (an inherited blood condition).

The public was asked to come in for testing for HIV, but some people were afraid. And, as with other sexually transmitted diseases, they were told to give the names of their partners to the health department.

This law was important to finding the spread of HIV. But, people still were afraid because they knew their jobs, their families, and their friends would not want them around. Some of these patients, who were tested, did lose their jobs and could not find any other. If the patient tested positive for HIV, then they would not be hired and otherwise discriminated against. Where was our right to privacy? Does it occur when serious diseases (another example: ebola) threaten to spread quickly?

But, how did the doctors, employers, and businesses find out the test results? Doctors could not give out this information, but, soon, they were required to by law, so the government could track the cases. Then, people were really frightened. But, the law did contain one thing: the results were sent with no names, only numbers, and *no* medical records were available.

Committees in the Center for Disease Control (CDC) were asked to find partners on the list and inform them of their danger, offer testing and follow-up.

In Illinois, a law was passed that anyone applying for a marriage license must present proof of taking an HIV test, but the results were not given to the state. So, what about the two people marrying? Did they have to tell each other?

At this point, we come upon the most striking of the problems: discrimination on every level. This topic had been faced in many venues: age, race, religion, monetary means, and many others. We are all familiar how it can applied in employment, marriage laws, and areas to live in. Where we, humans, were never sure how others would look at us or treat us.

Oddly enough, you did not even need an HIV diagnosis to be discriminated against.

Just to be in a group where HIV was prevalent, that was all you needed.

Remember the Tasmanian devil? Would this work for people?

Case 2: Ryan White: Discrimination

Ryan White was an American teenager from Indiana, who became a national poster child for HIV/AIDS in the United States after failing to be re-admitted to school following a diagnosis of AIDS. As a hemophiliac, he became infected with HIV from a contaminated factor VIII blood treatment,* and when diagnosed in December 1984, was given six months to live. Healthy for most of his childhood, White became extremely ill with pneumonia in December 1984 and was given a lung biopsy on December 17, 1984. White was diagnosed with AIDS. AIDS was poorly understood by the general public at the time.

When White tried to return to school, many parents and teachers rallied against his attendance due to concerns of the disease spreading. In addition, when the state announced he could return, that day no students or teachers came.

Before Ryan White, AIDS was a disease stigmatized as an illness impacting the gay community, because it was first diagnosed among gay men. That perception shifted as Ryan and other prominent straight HIV-infected people such as Magic Johnson (basketball), Arthur Ashe (tennis), and the Ray Brothers*† appeared in the media to advocate for more AIDS research and public education to address the epidemic. The United States passed a major piece of AIDS legislation, the Ryan White Care Act shortly after Ryan's death. The Act has been reauthorized twice.

Case 3: ACT UP (Grass Roots Organization): Getting Things Moving

The FDA (federal drug administration) through a time-consuming and costly process approves new drugs only after animal testing and four stages of human testing called clinical trials.

This process takes years and cost millions of dollars. So, what happens if a condition is life-threatening and affects many people?

In the 1980s, this was a situation where life was threatened because of HIV. Thousands of people were dying of AIDS, but the cost and the time commitment slowed down everything.

Leaders of an organization called ACT UP began using social activism to generate change, bring more drugs to the market, and increase the awareness about HIV. This small organization of gay men and women organized a grassroots movement to get AIDS into the national spotlight. How do you get the attention of the public?

In June 1989, one of the most successful protests was held in front of the Sloan Kettering Hospital in New York. Protesters dressed in healthcare worker's outfits and patients' outfits. They sat in front of the hospital for four days, while acting out scenarios about people dying of AIDS.

---

* Factor VIII is the blood component that helps the blood clot. Hemophilia has been known for many years due to the stories told about a Russian royal family (the Romanoffs) whose only son, Alexis, had the condition. Of course, no one understood what it was, and he was desperately ill. He was the heir to the throne. Oddly though, he did not die from the condition because his family was overthrown, and they all were killed in July 1918.

† The Ray brothers were three brothers diagnosed with HIV in 1986. The citizens of their small town burned their home.

The purpose of the protest was to demand that more people with HIV be included in the clinical trials for these drugs.

Because of the pressure brought about by ACT UP and other groups, the FDA was forced to make HIV drugs available for treatment under an already existing rule called "compassionate use rule" that allowed new drugs to be moved through the trials more quickly. This was the first step.

Finally, in 1997, the FDA formally introduced the fast-track designation and priority review for HIV and other fatal diseases.

Case 4: HIV in the Blood Supply: 1980s

It was known early on that HIV was a blood-borne disease, but for some reason, the medical community did not see this as a danger to the donated blood supply. People with HIV continued donating their blood without a thought (most did not know they were infected). After patients with HIV, who did not fit into known groups, were found to have the virus, the American Red Cross was alarmed and demanded testing of all blood that was donated. Law suits were filed for negligence, but they were dropped. Soon a full scale plan to test blood donations before they were put to use, using no name, sex or area of the country.

Case 5: Does the Government Have an Obligation to Protect Its Citizens?

According to the constitution of most states, they do. If an epidemic (such as HIV) enters our country, what does protection mean? Place those with the virus in areas and give them everything they need.

This would mean finding out who is infected and placing them in a "safe" place until they could be "cured."

Timeline of an Epidemic

As of now,

- 1978: early case of AIDS in the United States (baby born to a 16-year-old drug user)
- 1980: a case of Kaposi's sarcoma* in San Francisco (first case in the United States)
- March 7, 1980: headline in NYT reads: Rare Cancer Seen in 41 gay men.
- July 4, 1980: clusters of opportunistic conditions* reported.
- By the end of 1980: 121 men have died.
- 1982: first cases in Spain, United Kingdom, Italy, Brazil, Canada, and Australia.
- 1983: a retrovirus identified as HTLV-I and then HIV is the cause.
- 1983: Blood donor screening guidelines (includes high-risk groups excluded from giving blood).
- 1983: PCR invented by Kary Mullis, used in AIDS research.
- 1984: cases in Portugal, the Philippines, China, Soviet Union, Italy.
- Robert Gallo isolates HIV.
- December 17, 1984: Ryan White diagnosed with AIDS.
- March 12, 1985: ELISA test for HIV in the blood is available.
- 1986: one million Americans have been infected with HIV.
- 1987: first antiretroviral (treatment for HIV) becomes available.
- 1987: ELISA test gives rise to the Western Blot.
- March of 1987: ACT UP formed.*
- 1987: first clinical trial of AIDS vaccine.
- 1989: Film about the life of Ryan White, called the Ryan White Story, comes out.
- 1989: HIV was discovered in newborns.
- April 8, 1990: Ryan White dies.*
- Congress passes the Ryan White Care Act, which allotted funds for HIV.

- 1996: HIV-resistance gene (CCR5-D32) found.
- 1996: numbers of HIV patients is now 1.5 million.
- 2003: George Bush passes the Emergency Plan for AIDS relief.

Scientists have found the cause of HIV, how it was passed from monkeys to humans (eating monkey meat), how it was passed from human to human, and finally, treatment for it.

Now, HIV patients can live full lives and never move to AIDS.

The only thing left now was finding a prophylactic that would work to keep healthy people from contracting it. Is this impossible?

Yes, but I have a story. As you read it, think about this: if we could stop HIV, how much would it cost?

+++

Robert Grant had just finished medical school and one of his professors asked him, "What will you do now?"

The answer was: "HIV research."

The professor surprised him by saying "Do something else; by the time you are finished, the epidemic will be over."

Grant thought very seriously about this statement. He knew that working on a cure or a vaccine had been unsuccessful, but he had another idea.

The antivirals have been successful in keeping the viral low count, and even though you have to take them the rest of your life, you will not move into AIDS. Could these drugs be given to patients who did not have HIV and keep them clear.

He raised grant money from the governmental and private funds to finance his plan. What was his plan?

To run clinical trials with people who have never had or been exposed to HIV using an antiviral as a daily regimen. From the beginning, the study gave a drug to each of the participants. One pill per day.

The drug, trivada, was an antiviral already used in treatment along with other drugs to stop the virus from multiplying.

Trials were run for eight years, using trivada that was donated from its manufacturer. Each participant was tested for HIV and was found clear.

Then, every day, for eight years, these participants went about their day taking one pill every day, its name was PrEP (pre-exposure prophylaxis).

It worked! Not one of his participants on trivada contracted HIV. This was more than he imagined, but the story is not over yet.

Numbers

One person on Trivada from age 25–50 would need one pill a day, 365 pills a year, but it turned out that the drug was under patent. The company donated pills for the trial, but did not lower the cost to everyone.

Thousands of men, women, and drug users could use it without fear, but $14,000 U.S. dollars per year was impossible for most. The drug is out there and being taken by those who have insurance or can afford it. Dr. Grant had hoped everyone could take it and HIV would be only a memory.

CHAPTER 8

Allergies

What Causes Allergies?

Allergies results from the immune system's reaction to allergens; these are carried by dust or certain foods. One of the most serious food allergies are allergies to peanuts. Allergic reactions to peanuts, bee stings, and other allergies have very serious reactions. This reaction is called anaphylactic shock. If a patient is not given medicine immediately, they will die quickly because of this reaction. Parents with children that have this serious allergy must have an EpiPen with them at all times. 80% of all these serious allergy attacks are caused from peanuts. Children and adults with this allergy can die very quickly. Called anaphylaxis, it can occur during the FIRST exposure. Symptoms include swelling of the tongue and throat, constriction of the airway, and drop in blood pressure.

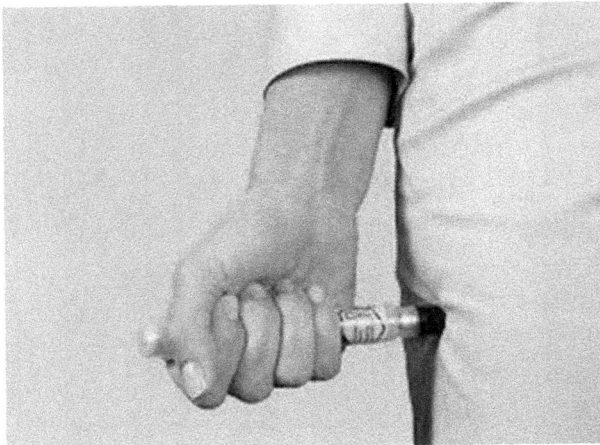

Figure 8.1 Patient giving himself an epinephrine shot. Needle is preset and doesn't need filling

This is so serious because only small amounts of the allergen needs to be present for the reaction to occur. One example is some schools do not allow anything that contains peanuts (even dust given off by the peanuts themselves).

Peanut allergies have increased since 2008: one percent of all children in the United States have these allergies to peanuts. People in countries that do not eat many peanuts (China) do not have these allergies. But in the United States children are exposed not only from what they eat, but from their mothers' breast milk. The reason for this seems to be two-fold and infants are very sensitive to these allergens. Doctors suggest that mothers not yet of their children have peanuts until they are older.

If you watch carefully, you may see signs in restaurants and other public places stating do not bring peanuts (Figure 8.2):

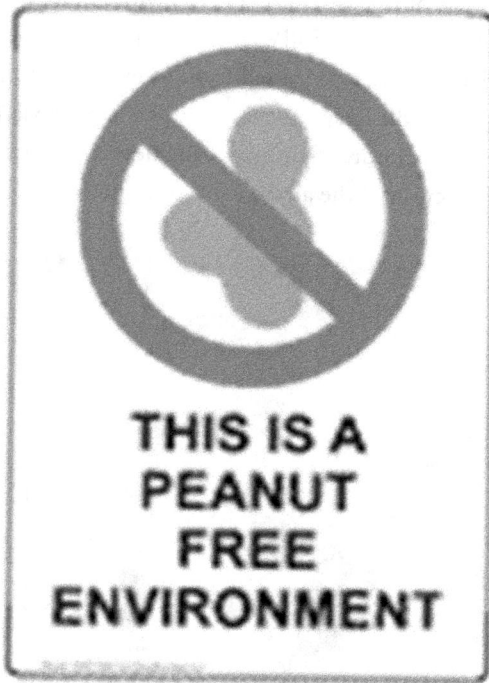

THIS IS A PEANUT FREE ENVIRONMENT

Figure 8.2 Peanut-free Sign in a Restaurant

Schools also have a problem if a child has a serious peanut allergy; they cannot be around any peanuts, and the schools must tell parents to send peanut butter and other foods with their children.

Just like autoimmune diseases, allergies are triggered by inflammation caused by foods, chemicals, air quality, formaldehyde (in new clothing and furniture), but allergies to peanuts are one of the most common ones in children and adults. It is estimated that 284.8 billion have allergies.

An interesting case: a baby was born with serious allergies to cow milk, and it was identified early. The mother, who was proud of her baby, took her to see a friend. When the friend kissed the baby after taking a sip of coffee with cream, the babies cheek swelled up in in shape of her friend's lips.

CHAPTER 9

Ethical and Legal Questions

Each of the topics we have covered has serious ethical questions that people (possibly you or your family) might encounter and how the law has addressed them.

Let us look at some of these:

Transplantation:

	Legal solution	Problem	Causes	Other
Donation	With permission, everyone	Donation low (see Chapter 4)	Lack of under-standing	A fiction book by Robin Cook called COMA (1977) fright-ened many[1]
When is the organ removed? Or When is death?	Time decided by patient's illness. Malpractice suits occur	When is the time of death?[2]	No one really knows when this is	Heart beat stops? Breathing stops? Brain death?
Who gets an organ?	The law sets guidelines	Someone might be pushed to #1[3]	Money, influence, celebrity	The organ donor data base is very careful.

[1] COMA was a book that set out a scenario where doctors kept patients in comas
[2] There have been times when 2 doctors needed to certify the time. A law suit for malpractice might be the result.
[3] In 1995, Mickey Mantle, a famous baseball hero died after two liver transplants. Many people thought they pushed him to the top of the list because of his fame.

Autoimmune conditions:

Where do they come from?	Diagnosis is difficult	Some suggest it is hereditary		Treatment is still not perfected
Family genetics	Many doctors have little knowledge	The basic symptom involves the immune system	Multiple symptoms from many organs make this	Uses immune suppressant drugs with many side effects

How to diagnose?	Specialized testing	Symptoms are similar to other illnesses	This is just becoming a medical specialty	One such condition, lupus[4] puzzled doctors for years
Can anyone get more than one?	Yes, often they develop over years.	Doctors often identified them as *stress related*	Patients were confused and often saw many doctors	

[4] Lupus (also called lupus erythematosus) has many symptoms. Some are: fatigue, rashes, hairloss, pain, seizures, and Raynaud's disese (constant cold in hands and feet)

Allergies:

Question:	When does it occur?	Problem	How to treat?	
Is this partially genetic?	Newborns to adult	Too many over-the-counter drugs available	Depends on symptoms (stuffed nose versus breathing stops)	Runs in families (for example, hay fever)
Fatal?	It could be. Serious reactions such as anaphylactic shock may prove fatal	Peanuts, shellfish	Keep away from peanuts or other allergens	Carry an EpiPen
Are they real?	Some say they are in the mind. But doctors do not agree.	This has been debunked.	Some of these diseases are long term and will not respond to medicines.	The symptoms can come and go Specialists called allergists can treat with allergy shots

HIV/AIDS:

Question:				
What has happened?	Safe sex and anti-viral treatments give a person a much longer life	Many famous celebrities came forward and urged people to get tested	Although the HIV virus had a stigma attached to it, Society needed time to understand the HIV virus was an illness	

Blood transfusions	At first, people with HIV were donating blood	Then, certain groups were identified and could not donate.	But later, a test of the donated blood came available	Still, many donors are refused.
Treatments	They are complex (anti-viral and life-long regimen)	Constant checking asymptomatic patient to keep a history in case symptoms appear	Still, the AIDS virus is mutating, so it is not over	A vaccine has not been developed due to mutations
Non-medical problems	Homosexuals were horribly treated even if they were clear	Many people were not *hired* because they were *suspected* of being gay	AIDS medication is amazingly expensive. Not available there.	Many wonderful and creative people died from this.

CHAPTER 10

What Would You Do If?

These little charts ask you to think of some of the scenarios this book presents and put yourself there. Maybe it will help to see my opinions and why I chose them.

Transplantation:

What would do if...	You	Me	My reason
Needed a kidney?		Look for a living donor (organ donor website).	Going on line or asking someone if they would consider giving would be the way to go for me, the person you speak to might feel guilty.
You wanted to talk to your family about donation after death?		There are forms called informed consent. I have already done this[1].	Just say "let us look at this form." this does not have to be a spouse or friend, a doctor might help and, read it together, talk a lot.
You wanted to donate your organs after death?		*Yes*, without hesitation (I indicate such on my driver's license).	It is a wonderful way to help people and the environment.

---

[1] I was very affected by a case where a young woman, engaged to be married, was in a car accident and needed a respirator to breathe. Her parents and her fiancé did not feel the same way. The parents thought she should stay on the respirator because they knew she would wake up. But, the fiancé said that he was told, by her, that she did not want to be on a respirator. But, no written document existed. Two groups picketed the hospital: church groups and people who felt she had a right to a death of her choosing. The court found for the fiancé.

[2] Note: the HIV test cost 100 U.S. dollars each and the marriage license was five U.S. dollars. We were both negative.

Take an HIV test if asked to by a friend?		Well, when I got married, Illinois was the only state to mandate an HIV test for a marriage license.	Oddly enough, no results had to be shown; just the form signed by a doctor stating the test was given[2].
Ask a friend if they were HIV positive?		This is hard, I am not sure; it does not seem to be my business.	This would be something you could ask a significant other.
Tell a person about the importance of vaccines.		Give them an article to read and point out in simple terms why this cannot be connected with another disease (autism).	Hard to do due to the lack of basic science education..
You were asked to donate bone marrow to a child with leukemia.		Yes, it would be hard to say no. We all would like to help.	Bone marrow extraction is not really that bad.

Bibliography

Cummings, M. 2017. *Human Heredity.*

Grady, D. December 5, 2017. *Woman With Transplanted Uterus Gives Birth, the First in the U.S.* NYT.

Hole, A. 2016. "Let People Sell their Organs." *Fortune Magazine.*

Kolata, G. March 9, 2016. *New Procedure Allows Kidney Transplants from Any Donor.* NYT.

Ofri, D. August 25, 2014. *Imagine a World Without AIDS.* NYT.

organdonor.gov. Organ Donation and Transplant statistics: Graph Data.

Podcast.app 2017. *The Daily, This Drug Could End HIV: Why Hasn't it?*

Surviving AIDS, www.Wikipedia.org

Timeline of HIV/AIDS, www.wikipedia.com

Yashon, R. 2014. *Landmark Legal Cases in Science,* 5th ed. RJ Publications.

Yashon, R., and M. Cummings. 2015. *Human Genetics and Society,* 2nd ed. Cengage Learning.

And if you have some time be sure to read:

Cook, R. *Coma.*

Cook, R. *Chromosome 6.*

About the Authors

Ronnee Yashon is a nationally known expert in teaching genetics, ethics, and the law on all levels. She has a background in teaching in the high school, undergraduate, graduate, and law school levels.

Her case study methodology for introducing bioethics and law, uses simple, personalized, and current scenarios that involve the students in decision making.

Michael R. Cummings is the author or coauthor of several college textbooks, including Human Heredity Principles and Issues, Concepts of Genetics, and Essentials of Genetics. He was a faculty member at the University of Illinois at Chicago for over 25 years.

Index

OTHER TITLES IN OUR HUMAN GENETICS AND SOCIETY COLLECTION

Ronnee Yashon, Editor

Genetic Testing: What Do We Know?
by Ronnee Yashon and Michael R. Cummings

Chromosomes
by Ronnee Yashon and Michael R. Cummings

Biotechnology
by Ronnee Yashon and Michael R. Cummings

DNA Forensics
by Ronnee Yashon and Michael R. Cummings

Momentum Press is one of the leading book publishers in the field of engineering, mathematics, health, and applied sciences. Momentum Press offers over 30 collections, including Aerospace, Biomedical, Civil, Environmental, Nanomaterials, Geotechnical, and many others.

Momentum Press is actively seeking collection editors as well as authors. For more information about becoming an MP author or collection editor, please visit http://www.momentumpress.net/contact

Announcing Digital Content Crafted by Librarians

Momentum Press offers digital content as authoritative treatments of advanced engineering topics by leaders in their field. Hosted on ebrary, MP provides practitioners, researchers, faculty, and students in engineering, science, and industry with innovative electronic content in sensors and controls engineering, advanced energy engineering, manufacturing, and materials science.

Momentum Press offers library-friendly terms:

- perpetual access for a one-time fee
- no subscriptions or access fees required
- unlimited concurrent usage permitted
- downloadable PDFs provided
- free MARC records included
- free trials

The **Momentum Press** digital library is very affordable, with no obligation to buy in future years.

For more information, please visit **www.momentumpress.net/library** or to set up a trial in the US, please contact **mpsales@globalepress.com.**